ALVIN AILEY

The **African-American Biographies** Series

MARIAN ANDERSON
Singer and Humanitarian
0-7660-1211-5

BENJAMIN BANNEKER
Astronomer and Mathematician
0-7660-1208-5

MARY McLEOD BETHUNE
Educator and Activist
0-7660-1771-0

JULIAN BOND
Civil Rights Activist and Chairman
of the NAACP
0-7660-1549-1

GEORGE WASHINGTON CARVER
Scientist and Inventor
0-7660-1770-2

BESSIE COLEMAN
First Black Woman Pilot
0-7660-1545-9

FREDERICK DOUGLASS
Speaking Out Against Slavery
0-7660-1773-7

DR. CHARLES DREW
Blood Bank Innovator
0-7660-2117-3

W.E.B. DU BOIS
Champion of Civil Rights
0-7660-1209-3

PAUL LAURENCE DUNBAR
Portrait of a Poet
0-7660-1350-2

MARCUS GARVEY
Controversial Champion
of Black Pride
0-7660-2168-8

NIKKI GIOVANNI
Poet of the People
0-7660-1238-7

WHOOPI GOLDBERG
Comedian and Movie Star
0-7660-1205-0

FANNIE LOU HAMER
Fighting for the Right to Vote
0-7660-1772-9

LORRAINE HANSBERRY
Playwright and Voice of Justice
0-89490-945-2

LANGSTON HUGHES
Poet of the Harlem Renaissance
0-89490-815-4

JESSE JACKSON
Civil Rights Activist
0-7660-1390-1

MAHALIA JACKSON
The Voice of Gospel and Civil Rights
0-7660-2115-7

QUINCY JONES
Musician, Composer, Producer
0-89490-814-6

MARTIN LUTHER KING, JR.
Leader for Civil Rights
0-89490-687-9

JOHN LEWIS
From Freedom Rider to
Congressman
0-7660-1768-0

THURGOOD MARSHALL
Civil Rights Attorney and
Supreme Court Justice
0-7660-1547-5

KWEISI MFUME
Congressman and NAACP Leader
0-7660-1237-9

WALTER DEAN MYERS
Writer for Real Teens
0-7660-1206-9

COLIN POWELL
Soldier and Patriot
0-89490-810-3

A. PHILIP RANDOLPH
Union Leader and Civil Rights
Crusader
0-7660-1544-0

PAUL ROBESON
Actor, Singer, Political Activist
0-89490-944-4

JACKIE ROBINSON
Baseball's Civil Rights Legend
0-89490-690-9

WILMA RUDOLPH
The Greatest Woman Sprinter
in History
0-7660-2291-9

BETTY SHABAZZ
Sharing the Vision
of Malcolm X
0-7660-1210-7

MARY CHURCH TERRELL
Speaking Out for Civil Rights
0-7660-2116-5

HARRIET TUBMAN
Moses of the Underground
Railroad
0-7660-1548-3

MADAM C. J. WALKER
Self-Made Businesswoman
0-7660-1204-2

DENZEL WASHINGTON
Academy Award–Winning Actor
0-7660-2131-9

CARTER G. WOODSON
Father of African-American History
0-89490-946-0

RICHARD WRIGHT
Author of *Native Son*
and *Black Boy*
0-7660-1769-9

—African-American Biographies—

ALVIN AILEY

Celebrating African-American Culture In Dance

Series Consultant:
Dr. Russell L. Adams, Chairman
Department of Afro-American Studies, Howard University

Bárbara C. Cruz

Enslow Publishers, Inc.

40 Industrial Road	PO Box 38
Box 398	Aldershot
Berkeley Heights, NJ 07922	Hants GU12 6BP
USA	UK

http://www.enslow.com

For my prima ballerinas:
Cristina, Amanda, Raquel, and Patricia

Library of Congress Cataloging-in-Publication Data

Cruz, Bárbara.
    Alvin Ailey : celebrating African-American culture in dance / Bárbara C. Cruz. — 1st ed.
        p. cm. — (African-American biographies)
    Includes bibliographical references and index.
    ISBN 0-7660-2293-5 (hardcover)
    1. Ailey, Alvin—Juvenile literature. 2. Dancers—United States—Biography—Juvenile literature. 3. Choreographers—United States—Biography—Juvenile literature. [1. Ailey, Alvin. 2. Dancers. 3. Choreographers. 4. African Americans—Biography. 5. Alvin Ailey American Dance Theater.] I. Title. II. Series.
    GV1785.A38C78   2004
    792.8'028'092—dc22
    [B]   2003026957

Printed in the United States of America

10 9 8 7 6 5 4 3 2

To Our Readers: We have done our best to make sure all Internet Addresses in this book were active and appropriate when we went to press. However, the author and the publisher have no control over and assume no liability for the material available on those Internet sites or on other Web sites they may link to. Any comments or suggestions can be sent by e-mail to comments@enslow.com or to the address on the back cover.

Every effort has been made to locate all copyright holders of material used in this book. If any errors or omissions have occurred, corrections will be made in future editions of this book.

Illustration Credits: Jerome Robbins Dance Division, The New York Public Library for Performing Arts, Astor, Lenox and Tilden Foundations, pp. 10, 36, 45, 55, 64, 76, 81; Kimberly D. Eazell, p. 92; Library of Congress, Prints and Photographs Division, pp. 15, 18, 24, 26, 28, 32, 40, 50, 57; Steve Dunwell, photographer, p. 87.

Cover Illustration: Library of Congress, Prints and Photographs Division.

CONTENTS

Acknowledgments

The author wishes to thank the following people:

Jason O'Brien and Jennifer Groendal,
for their research assistance;

John Parks, for his insights and generous
sharing of his time and resources;

Cristina E. Yelvington and Raquel L. Fariñas, for their
excellent editorial skills and constructive feedback;

The anonymous reviewers,
for their thorough and helpful comments;

And, of course, Kevin A. Yelvington,
for his unwavering support and encouragement.

1

BLUES SUITE

he auditorium at the Young Men's and Young Women's Hebrew Association was filled with dancers, actors, and choreographers. They had come to the 92nd Street YM-YWHA in New York City to see a special dance performance. The year was 1958, and the Y had become the city's center for modern dance. Just about every night, audiences were treated to the latest works by a variety of new young choreographers.

The thirty-five dancers on the program that night—all African American—had worked hard to get ready. Although they were not a real dance company, they were joined by their common desire to create a new dance style. The group was operating on a shoestring budget, so everyone had pitched in to create the scenery, gather props, and set the stage. The costumes were assembled from items found at the Salvation Army secondhand store.

The twenty-six-year-old choreographer and lead dancer, Alvin Ailey Jr., did not have much experience. For a professional dancer, he had gotten a late start. Ailey had never even seen a professional dance performance until he was a teenager. He was eighteen years old before he had any dance training. Still, after that he wasted no time in catching up.

Ailey had started choreographing—that is, composing and arranging dances—in 1953, just five years before his show at the Y. On this night, he would have the opportunity to present some very special dances of his own creation.

The performance started with *Redonda (Five Dances on Latin Themes)*. The inspiration for *Redonda* had come from movements found in Caribbean, Brazilian, and African dance styles. Some of the dances in *Redonda*, such as "El Cigaro" (the cigar), had storylines that kept the audience enthralled.

Next, Ailey performed a long solo dance dedicated to his teacher Lester Horton, who had died five years earlier. The solo, *Ode and Homage*, was described in the program as a "dance of faith." One dance critic said that while Ailey's *Ode and Homage* "revealed a lack of experience, . . . [it] had an inherent nobility"—a natural grace that was evident in the dance.[1]

The show ended with a unique number called *Blues Suite.* For this piece, the stage of the Kaufmann Auditorium was transformed into a dance hall. The female dancers wore slinky, ruffled dresses, stockings, and high-heeled shoes. The men were dressed in street clothing and sported hats that hung over one eye. These images were drawn from Ailey's childhood memories of the Dew Drop Inn, a Texas bar and dance hall where people gathered on Saturday nights. As a child, Ailey would sneak around to one of the back windows of the inn to watch the Saturday night drama unfold before his eyes. Inside, people were dancing, laughing, and occasionally fighting.

Blues Suite is set to blues music, an original American music style. The dance depicts African-American life in a small town, yet everyone can relate to emotions that are common to all human beings— anguish, defeat, and triumph. The audience at the Y came away with a sense of the African-American struggle to overcome hardships and hopelessness. As one writer said, "Escaping the magnetic pull of the blues danced Ailey style was rare, if not impossible. No one was exempt from the pull of Ailey's choreographic magnetism."[2]

More than just a dance, *Blues Suite* is like a miniplay.

Alvin, top left, and Nathaniel Horne, Minnie Marshall, Merle Derby, and Barbara Alston in *Blues Suite*. Alvin created this original piece from memories of his childhood in Texas.

Every dancer has a role to act. As one of his dancers put it, "He [Ailey] didn't want you to just come out there and do the steps. He wanted a reason behind it."[3] In Ailey's choreographies, every detail was researched to understand the history behind the work. Ailey told his dancers, "You don't move unless you have a reason."[4]

The dancers who performed that night had jobs in other shows and clubs. They had rehearsed and worked with Ailey purely out of their love for dance. One dancer said of Ailey, "He had the knack of making you tear your guts out onstage. You really wanted to give it all you had."[5] Ailey paid the dancers as much as he could afford: $5 each.[6]

By all accounts, the performance was a success. The dance critic Doris Hering proclaimed, "As a dancer, Mr. Ailey is exceptional. He reminds one of a caged lion full of lashing power that he can contain or release at will."[7]

The dance troupe was invited to perform again at the YM-YWHA before the end of the year. Later, Ailey said that the 1958 performances were part of his "apprentice years," the time when he was in training to be the director of a dance company.[8]

Little did Ailey—or the dance world—know that he was beginning a thirty-year career that would revolutionize American dance.

2

THE BIRTH
OF A DANCER

lvin Ailey was born on January 5, 1931, in the rural town of Rogers, Texas. His mother, Lula Elizabeth Ailey, was just sixteen years old. Alvin later described her as a "gorgeous, caring, daring, fascinating, sensible, religious, theatrical woman with a great sense of humor and leadership ability."[1] All his life, Alvin would have a deep love and respect for his mother.

Alvin was born during the Great Depression. This period of history—from 1929 to about 1940—was marked by a severe economic decline in most of the industrialized world. In the United States, thousands of Americans lost their jobs and their homes. As people used up all their savings, charities strained to help millions of Americans with the basic necessities of food, clothing, and shelter.

For African Americans, life during the depression was especially hard. When work became scarce, black people were often forced out of their jobs so that whites could be hired instead. In addition to the economic hardships, African Americans faced segregation in every aspect of their lives. Local and national laws made it legal to exclude African Americans from many public places. Blacks and whites could not mix with one another in schools, churches, theaters, and neighborhoods. Racism and prejudice were bitter parts of everyday life.

Lula had married Alvin Ailey Sr. in 1929. At first the newlyweds lived with Lula's father. Then they moved in with Alvin Sr.'s father, Henry Ailey. Thirteen family members all lived together in one dilapidated house.

The winter Alvin Jr. was born was bitterly cold. A harsh wind blew through the cracks in the walls as Lula was giving birth. The bare room held only a pot-bellied stove, a bed for Lula, and a cot for the doctor. All through her pregnancy, Lula had worried about the health of her baby because she did not feel him moving inside her. She was greatly relieved to find her son alert and curious just a few hours after birth.[2]

Food in the household was scarce, and Lula was so malnourished that she was unable to produce milk for her infant. She fed baby Alvin a mixture of water and sugar until he was able to eat table food.

When Alvin Jr. was three months old, he and his parents moved out of the crowded house into their own one-room cabin. It was a difficult life, and when the baby turned six months old, Alvin Sr. abandoned his family. Lula soon started taking in washing and ironing from some white families who lived nearby. Although she did not earn much, the money helped to provide for herself and her baby. Lula's vegetable garden also put food on their table.

Alvin was a big baby with a large appetite. He did not walk on his own until he was eighteen months old.[3] Still, he managed to get into trouble in his early years. One day, Lula had to leave Alvin alone. She instructed him not to touch the beans she was cooking for dinner. Alvin's hunger got the better of him, though, and he ate an enormous amount of half-cooked beans. That night, Alvin groaned in pain, his stomach sore and swollen. Carrying the child on her back, Lula walked eight miles to the nearest doctor. A strong dose of castor oil proved to be all he needed.[4]

In search of work in 1935, Lula Ailey and her four-year-old son boarded a train for Wharton, Texas. They arrived in time for the cotton harvest. Both Alvin and his mother picked cotton to earn money. Alvin later

Like this woman in Beaumont, Texas, Alvin's mother earned money by
washing clothes for other people.

remembered, "When we left the cotton fields at sunset, I would sit on one of the wagons and ride home. I remember the people moving in the twilight back to their little shacks."[5]

When they returned to Rogers, Texas, in 1936, Alvin was almost five years old. He later described the town of his birth as "small, mean-spirited, dirt-poor, and racist."[6] He said, "I have deep memories of the situation there [in Rogers, Texas] . . . sharecropping, picking cotton, people being lynched, all the Black men having been to prison, segregated schools, movie theatres where I had to sit in the balcony."[7] These unpleasant recollections would stay with him for the rest of his life.

In Rogers, Alvin and his mother moved into the house of Alvin's aunt Nettie. Alvin began attending school with Nettie's twins. He soon proved to be a quick learner, mastering his multiplication tables up to five.

Alvin also became close to a Mexican family. Through his friendship with one of the boys, Manuel, Alvin learned to speak Spanish. His gift for learning languages would be important later in his life.

Lula Ailey heard that there was a new highway being built in Navasota, Texas, and she went looking for a job there. She was hired to cook lunches for the work crew and found a home on the property of Amos Alexander, who was quite wealthy for an African

American. Alexander took a liking to Alvin, and they became close, as if they were father and son. Alvin was assigned regular chores, learned how to ride a horse, and got his first dog. He started going to the Navasota Colored School, one of the first African-American schools to have a music program. It was a happy, stable time for Alvin.

After six months in Navasota, Lula Ailey suddenly became very sick. She needed emergency surgery to remove her appendix. At that time, hospitals were for white patients only. Blacks were treated as outpatients, and they were not allowed to stay overnight. An exception was made for Alvin's mother.

For the first time in Navasota's history, an African-American patient was admitted to the hospital. To help pay for her surgery and hospital expenses, the doctors offered Lula a job in their medical clinic. After she recovered, she became the first African American employed by the Navasota Hospital. Her duties included caring for elderly patients and sterilizing surgical tools.

Life settled into a predictable and enjoyable rhythm for young Alvin. He was never without "Big Ben"—a large notebook in which he wrote and drew things he observed and encountered. Scribbling in notebooks became a lifelong habit, and his musings and memories would later serve as important creative inspiration for his work.

This five-year-old child in Texas is picking cotton, just like young Alvin, who worked in the fields alongside his mother.

On Saturday nights, many of the town's citizens went out to socialize. African Americans had their own clubs and gathering places. One place in particular, the Dew Drop Inn, made an impact on Alvin, who later described it as a "Honky-Tonk" nightclub with music and dancing and "an atmosphere of sensuality always accompanied by fear or a sense of impending trouble."[8] One minute there would be laughing, music, and dancing. The next minute, a sudden argument might escalate into a fight. The tension-filled mood of these scenes later became the basis for the ballet *Blues Suite*.

On Sundays, the Aileys spent most of their day in church, with services and Sunday school at the True Vine Baptist Church, a congregation composed entirely of African Americans. Some of the sounds and sights that Alvin experienced proved to be powerful, inspirational memories later on in his life. One of the most impressive was the baptism ceremony that was held in a nearby river, with parishioners dressed all in white singing and clapping their way down to the water's edge. These images would later become part of *Revelations*, one of Ailey's most famous dance pieces.

Despite the fond childhood memories that Ailey would write about in his autobiography, he was also aware of difficult times. He knew that African Americans were not treated fairly. In addition to the economic difficulties and the segregation, there were lynchings of African Americans by mobs that took the law into their own hands. Without a trial or even a chance to tell their side of the story, African Americans accused of crimes were executed. Often they were tortured first, then put to death by hanging.

Schooling for African Americans was also far from equal—and in certain places it was just about nonexistent. There were not many opportunities for African-American children to experience art, music, theater, or dance. Ailey said, "There was a white school up on the hill, and the black Baptist church and the segregated theaters and neighborhoods. Like most of my generation, I grew up feeling like an outsider, like someone who didn't matter."[9]

Alvin's life changed again when his mother decided to move to Los Angeles in 1942. The United States was in the throes of World War II, a conflict that affected almost every country in the world. The war had begun in 1939. It was being fought across the ocean in Europe, and at first the United States was not involved. Then, in 1941, the Japanese bombed the U.S. naval base at Pearl Harbor, Hawaii, and the United States sent troops to Europe to fight.

The war had stimulated the aircraft industry in California, and Lula Ailey heard there were good job opportunities. At first she found work as a housekeeper in an expensive apartment house. She and Alvin moved into the building's four-room basement apartment. This living arrangement did not last, however. Alvin was unhappy at the local junior high school, which was integrated. Unaccustomed to attending school with white children, he felt alone and isolated. Soon, his mother found an apartment in a mostly black neighborhood of Los Angeles. She took a job at the Lockheed factory, where airplanes were being manufactured for the war.

Alvin liked his new school, George Washington Carver Junior High. The student body was a mix of

African Americans, Asians, and Hispanics. Alvin's early aptitude for Spanish paid off: He did so well in his Spanish course that his teacher sometimes allowed him to teach the class.[10] Alvin started thinking about becoming a foreign-language teacher when he grew up.

Alvin joined the glee club and learned more about music and singing. His teacher introduced him to the music of William S. Gilbert and Arthur S. Sullivan, who had created popular operettas at the start of the twentieth century. *The Pirates of Penzance*, *Princess Ida*, and *HMS Pinafore* were easily understood and enjoyed by the public. Alvin was awed by Gilbert and Sullivan's *The Mikado*.

Alvin also explored dance. Although he tried tap dancing, he did not care much for it and quit the lessons after two months. His mother was not happy that the $35 she had spent for tap shoes was wasted.

In 1945 Alvin's mother remarried. Fred Cooper was a sailor stationed at the nearby naval base in Oxnard. He was a quiet man whose shyness frustrated Lula, although she appreciated the fact that he cared for her son.[11] Fourteen-year-old Alvin was not happy about the marriage. He was jealous of the time that his mother was spending with her new husband. He later wrote, "I couldn't stand him at first because I thought he was demanding and getting all my mother's attention."[12] After a while, though, Alvin got used to Fred Cooper and developed a good relationship with his stepfather. Alvin was happy when his mother later had another son, Calvin.

In the fall of 1945, Alvin started attending Thomas Jefferson Senior High School. Although he tried to participate in football and track, he did not like the competitive nature of these sports. Instead, he took up gymnastics. His favorite part of gymnastics was the freestyle floor exercises, which had similarities to dance. This interest in dance-style movement was a hint of great things to come.

3

Discovering
Dance

n a junior high school field trip to Los Angeles, Alvin had seen the visiting Ballet Russe de Monte Carlo. Although he was impressed with their performance of the exotic and lavish *Scheherazade*, he was disappointed by the rest of the program, which he found unexciting. The best part of the trip was discovering the city's theater district. Soon, Alvin started taking bus trips into the city on Saturdays while his mother worked.[1] At the movies and in theaters, Alvin saw great African-American performers, such as the jazz singer Billie Holiday and the popular singers Pearl Bailey and Lena Horne, who

Alvin was drawn to the rhythms of Duke Ellington's jazz music.

also acted in plays and musicals. He also discovered the big-band jazz music of Duke Ellington, a gifted composer and bandleader. Later in his life, Alvin would pay tribute to Ellington with a dance piece.

Alvin became more aware of dance by watching movies starring Fred Astaire and Gene Kelly. These multitalented American actors made films that showcased an athletic style of dance. *The Sky's the Limit, Holiday Inn, Ziegfeld Follies,* and other movies introduced Alvin to the possibility of men as professional dancers. At home, he imitated dance steps that he had seen in the films. He was particularly impressed by the fact that there were *men* in leading dance roles; he had always thought of dancers as women. Still, he was sensitive to the fact that male dancers were sometimes called sissies, so he kept his growing interest to himself.

One day, Alvin was surprised to see an advertisement for a dance company made up entirely of African Americans. His curiosity led him to the Katherine Dunham Dance Company's *Tropical Revue* at the Biltmore Theater in downtown Los Angeles.

Dunham was an African-American dancer and choreographer who was also an anthropologist—a person who studies the history, development, and customs of human cultures. While majoring in anthropology at the University of Chicago, she also continued dancing. Dunham went on to study anthropology and dance in the Caribbean. These cultural studies influenced her

Seeing gifted actors like Gene Kelly, above, opened Alvin's eyes to the idea that men could be dancers.

choreography and led to lavish, colorful dance reviews such as *Caribbean Rhapsody*, *Carib Song*, and *Bal Nègre*. Dunham's work reflected the Afro-Caribbean rhythms, scenery, and costumes that she encountered in her travels. When her dance company toured Europe in the late 1940s, it was the first time Europeans had seen African-American dance as an art form.

Alvin was awestruck by the Dunham dancers and the performance. He said of that experience, "I was lifted up into another realm. I couldn't believe there were black people on a legitimate stage in downtown Los Angeles, before largely white audiences, being appreciated for their artistry."[2]

Alvin and his high school friend Ted Crumb found out where the Dunham company was rehearsing and began sneaking in to watch. One of the lead dancers, Lucille Ellis, befriended Alvin and took him backstage to the dressing rooms. Alvin was amazed by all the color and activity—dancers touching up their shoes, pressing their costumes, and bustling about. Sometimes he would pass by Dunham's dressing room, hoping to catch sight of her. Later Alvin said, "I was completely hooked from the moment I saw those beautiful Black dancers doing dances taken from all over the world."[3]

As exciting as the experience with Dunham's company had been, it was a school show that would ultimately change Alvin's life. He saw a fellow student perform a dance from *Scheherazade*, a ballet based on

Studying anthropology allowed Katherine Dunham, above, to understand the cultural origins of African-American dance styles.

the ancient Middle Eastern tale *The Thousand and One Nights*. The ballet centers on a beautiful slave named Zobeide and is danced to an explosive score by the Russian composer Nikolay Rimsky-Korsakov. The young woman dancer, Carmen de Lavallade, dressed in red, took Alvin's breath away. He exclaimed, "Anybody who could move around on her toes like that was capable of performing miracles."[4]

Carmen de Lavallade later saw Alvin at gymnastics. She invited him to sit in on one of the classes she was taking at Lester Horton's dance studio in nearby Hollywood. Alvin assured her he would come.

Meanwhile, Alvin's friend Ted had just been to a dance class and learned some new movements. Ted showed Alvin how to contract his torso, fall and roll on the floor, and express emotion through movement. Alvin was thrilled to see such exciting and different ways to move. Coincidentally, it turned out that Ted's class was at the Lester Horton Dance Theater. Alvin knew at that moment that he had to go to the dance studio and see it for himself.

4

LESTER'S PLACE

As soon as Alvin walked through the double doors of the dance studio, he knew he had found a place where he belonged. Here, he could learn more about his growing interest in dance. At 7566 Melrose in Hollywood, tucked between a repair shop and a bar, stood the Lester Horton Dance Theater, its bright yellow sign contrasting with the rich brown walls of the building. In addition to classrooms, the building also housed a small theater with 133 seats painted in a variety of colors. There was a room for stage scenery and props and one for costumes. Alvin was awed by all he saw.

In addition to his high school buddy Ted Crumb, Alvin knew some of the other people in the dance classes there. He recognized Carmen de Lavallade and another black dancer, James Truitte. At the time, few dance schools accepted African Americans. Alvin saw Hispanic and Asian dancers, too. In a society where so many institutions were still segregated, Lester Horton's dance studio was beautifully integrated. He later said of his teacher, "Lester let us know that we were *all* beautiful. There were Japanese and Mexicans and blacks, whites, greens, and pinks."[1]

Alvin was much too shy at first to participate in any of the dancing. He just sat in the back, studying the dancers' movements and watching the company rehearse for performances. After about a month, he decided to take the plunge and enroll in classes himself. He took an instant liking to Horton's technique and dance style.

Lester Horton had not had much formal dance training. Perhaps that is why he had a special understanding of Ailey's reserve. A native of Indiana, born in 1906, Horton had taken dance classes only occasionally. In the 1920s, when Horton was a young man, studying dance was not common for boys. Horton was also captivated by Native American culture and spent a considerable amount of time studying with American Indians. The deep respect he developed for all cultural

Ailey said he "nearly fainted" from surprise and delight the first time he saw the expressive movements of modern dance.

traditions was reflected in his dances with special movements, music, and costumes.

Eventually, Horton followed his dreams of theater and dance and studied with the famed Denishawn company of modern dance. Founded by Ruth St. Denis and Ted Shawn, this groundbreaking troupe had introduced America to a new kind of dance that was much less formal and much more exciting than traditional ballet. A dance teacher who had studied and performed with Denishawn took Horton on as a student. Performing in local arts shows, Horton soon began to develop his own style—a style that increased dancers' traditional movements and reflected Horton's interest in culture, history, and ethnic dance.

In 1932, after moving to California, Horton started putting together his own dance company. However, it was not until 1946 that he would establish his dance theater in Hollywood. Horton choreographed, taught classes, and performed. He was a demanding teacher, expecting his students to push themselves to their limits. In addition to the requirement of taking two or three classes each day, Horton's company often rehearsed for ten to twelve hours straight.[2] Bella Lewitzky, a principal dancer in the company, said, "We had a technique class twice daily and composition class every day. We had classes in current events. We became very concerned about what was going on in the world around us, and we danced about it."[3]

Besides being a fine dancer and choreographer, Horton paid attention to theatrics—that is, the sets, costumes, makeup, lighting, and acting. He instructed his dance students on the importance of lighting, scenery, costuming, and theatrical makeup. Horton's students participated in all aspects of production, including set design, publicity, and the running of a studio. They also made costumes, painted scenery, and installed lights. All of Ailey's pieces reflect this theatrical training.

Horton's company toured and performed mostly on the West Coast. In addition to arranging artistic dance pieces, Horton was able to choreograph popular dances. His success led to opportunities to choreograph musical numbers for films.

In 1944 Horton suffered a neck injury that caused him to stop dancing. He continued to choreograph and teach, however, and soon developed what is now known as the Horton technique. Horton's style is characterized by a strong torso (upper part of the body), sharp movements, and isolations (the movement of only one part of the body at a time). Every single muscle in the body is stretched and exercised. Along with the more typical exercises for legs and arms, Horton created exercises for shoulders, fingers, wrists, neck, ribs, and eyes. Slow stretches, swings, squats, and lunges all combine to dramatic effect and promote a dancer's agility, strength, and flexibility.

Ailey and the other dancers were also attracted to Horton because he treated the dance company as if it were a family. Having a multiracial cast of dancers was unheard of at the time. Just as most public institutions were still segregated, so were dance studios. Many of the dancers lived at Horton's house, most of them sharing meals there as well. Ailey said he thought of Horton "as a kind of father figure, a person who designed, choreographed, pushed everybody, developed young talent, and ran a company."[4]

"Lester Horton was the greatest influence of my career," said Ailey. "He is the reason I do all this. . . . When you came into the world of Lester Horton you came into a completely creative environment—people of all colors, music of all nations."[5]

Horton was known for his generosity. He awarded so many scholarships that the studio often did not have enough money. In the early stages of his dance company, Horton even lived at the studio to save money.

Horton's studio specialized in modern dance, which is a uniquely American dance form. Much less rigid and formal than ballet, modern dance has its origins at the beginning of the twentieth century, when dancers such as Isadora Duncan, Ruth St. Denis, and Martha Graham wanted to create a dance form that could freely express human emotions. They also choreographed dances that explored social themes. Whereas ballet emphasizes movements in the arms and legs,

Alvin in the "Rite" sequence from *Cinco Latinos*. Ailey's creativity and natural talent blossomed at the Horton School. In dancing, he said, he finally found something he "could not live without."

modern dance stresses the torso and is often danced barefoot.

After graduating from high school in 1948, Ailey enrolled at the University of California, Los Angeles. There he majored in Romance languages. He was already very good in Spanish and had also taken up French and Italian.

It was a grueling schedule for the young college student. The bus ride took two hours each way; Ailey left home at 6 A.M. and did not return until 7 P.M. He had no time to fit in classes at Horton's studio, which was an hour and a half away in Hollywood.

In the spring of 1949, Horton contacted Ailey to ask about his absence from the dance studio. Ailey described his exhausting school schedule and also said that he could not afford to pay for dance classes. Convinced that Ailey had true talent and desire, Horton offered him a scholarship. In exchange for working at the dance studio as a handyman, Ailey could take what-ever dance classes his college schedule permitted. To help pay his bills, Ailey also took a job at a nearby restaurant.

As the draining schedule caught up with Ailey, his grades began to suffer. At the end of the spring, he decided not to take any summer college classes. Instead, Ailey began to take dance classes at Horton's studio in earnest. Later, he recalled that summer fondly:

It was all very confusing, but I loved being at Lester's; he was making dances, and clothes, and doing very creative things. He was always encouraging to me and I became involved in a [dance] composition class in which I completed my first study.[6]

Still, Ailey did not expect to become a professional dancer. "I didn't really see myself as a dancer," he said. "I mean, what would I dance? It was 1949. A man didn't just become a dancer. Especially a black man."[7] So Ailey decided to leave dance and concentrate on getting his college degree.

In the fall of 1949, Ailey moved to San Francisco, California, and resumed his college education. He continued his studies in Romance languages at San Francisco State College. After a full day of school, Ailey worked at the Greyhound bus station, loading luggage from 4 P.M. until midnight. His classes began at eight the next morning.

It proved to be very lucky for Ailey that health insurance came with the job at Greyhound. Just a few months after moving to San Francisco, he had to undergo surgery to remove one of his kidneys. Ailey was young and strong, and he recuperated quickly.

In the spring of 1950, Ailey developed a friendship with a tall, young dancer named Marguerite Angelos, who was to be his first dance partner. Marguerite would later become famous as the great poet Maya Angelou. She is well known for her book *I Know*

Why the Caged Bird Sings, which gained international acclaim.

Angelos introduced Ailey to Lou Fontaine, a dancer and choreographer whose group performed at the Champagne Supper Club in downtown San Francisco. Fontaine invited Ailey to audition for the act, and he was hired immediately. Ailey, who was still not confident about his own skill as a dancer, said later, "I am sure that it was because Fontaine needed a male dancer—*any* male dancer."[8]

Several weeks after Ailey had been performing with Fontaine, the group was booked to perform in Los Angeles. While there, Ailey paid a visit to Horton's dance studio. That visit proved to be life changing:

> I was stunned when I saw a whole suite of Latin dances with the big skirts and everything. That did it—I returned to San Francisco and packed all of my things and moved back to Los Angeles. I went straight to the Horton School and began serious study. I had finally discovered that this was what I wanted and that I could not live without it.[9]

Ailey soon began a course of study that included daily classes in dance technique, art, drama, music, and practice for various shows. It was a happy and creative time for Ailey and the other dancers. But it came to an abrupt halt when they received devastating news on November 2, 1953: Lester Horton had had a fatal heart attack.

The troupe decided that Horton would have wanted

Ailey developed a friendship—and a dance number—with Marguerite Angelos, the future poet Maya Angelou.

them to keep the dance company alive. While they quickly found a manager, they still needed to find a choreographer.

Carmen de Lavallade remembered what happened next: "Alvin has always been a creative person so, naturally, it seemed reasonable that he would be the one to assume the role of choreographer for the company."[10] Before his death, Horton had sensed Ailey's leadership qualities.[11] In many ways, Ailey became the logical choice to lead the group.

Ailey was nervous about his new position as company director. The night before his first rehearsal, scheduled early in the morning, he slept in the studio to be certain he would not be late.[12]

Ailey created his first work of choreography, *According to St. Francis,* to honor his mentor and teacher, Lester Horton. St Francis of Assisi, in the thirteenth century, lived his beliefs: "Where there is hatred, let me sow love. . . . It is in giving that we receive."[13] Lester Horton had been a creative, generous, caring man who brought together dancers of all races and backgrounds and nurtured their talents.

At first, the piece was an hour long. But after suggestions from his fellow dancers, Ailey pared it down to a fifty-minute ballet with a thirty-four-minute main solo. The solo was so strenuous, Ailey guessed that the principal dancer, James Truitte, must have lost twenty-five pounds in the course of performances of this piece. Ailey called it a "kitchen-sink ballet" because it contained everything he could possibly think of.[14] The dance, which likens Horton to St. Francis of Assisi, celebrates faith and spiritual liberation. Big trees made out of plaster and draped with fabric served as the scenery.

Working in his mentor's shadow, Ailey said, "[I] felt I had to be the same kind of artist Lester was. I designed the sets, I designed the costumes, I did it all."[15] It was scary and exhilarating for the young dancer. Would dance audiences like his creations?

5

ON HIS OWN

efore Lester Horton's death, his dance company had been invited to the Jacob's Pillow Dance Festival held every summer in Lenox, Massachusetts. Now, as the new director, Ailey decided the troupe would perform *According to St. Francis* as a tribute to Horton's memory. About a dozen members of the dance troupe piled their scenery and costumes into two cars and a station wagon and drove across the country to Massachusetts. *St. Francis*, Ailey's first choreography, premiered June 1954 at the festival, along with some other pieces.

Ted Shawn, director of the festival and a pioneer

in modern dance, was unimpressed by Ailey's work. Shawn felt that Ailey's pieces were unfinished and too long. After the festival, he wrote a letter to the Horton school's business manager, Frank Eng, saying, "How dare you send this young man with these long ballets that have no form."[1] A review by the influential dance critic Walter Terry was also negative. Terry wrote that *According to St. Francis* was filled with "meaningless movement" and "was more sleep-inviting than stirring."[2]

Despite this discouraging feedback, Ailey was unfazed. He knew that he was still an apprentice learning his craft. Later that year Ailey received an opportunity he could not refuse. He and his high school friend Carmen de Lavallade were asked to dance in the movie *Carmen Jones,* which featured an African-American cast. For this film adaptation of the tragic opera *Carmen,* the story was updated and set in a World War II parachute factory. The actress Dorothy Dandridge received an Academy Award nomination for her performance opposite the male lead, Harry Belafonte.

One of the film's directors took note of Ailey and de Lavallade and asked the pair to perform as lead dancers in *House of Flowers.* This Broadway musical was based on a short story by the famous author Truman Capote. Set on a Caribbean island, the production featured a large African-American cast that included

Carmen de Lavallade remained Ailey's close friend for the rest of his life.

Pearl Bailey, Diahann Carroll, Geoffrey Holder, and Arthur Mitchell.

Up to this point, all that Ailey knew about dance he had learned from Horton. Ailey saw this invitation as an opportunity to learn from other teachers and choreographers and to expand his dance skills. Ailey and de Lavallade accepted and traveled to the East Coast to be in the show.

The show's choreographer, Herbert Ross, created a special solo for Ailey, called "Slide 'Boy' Slide." The number quickly became a favorite with the audience.[3] As the name implies, Ailey slid across the floor throughout the dance—on his knees as well as other parts of his body. On several occasions, Ailey moved with such energy that his pants split onstage. One night, he forgot to put on his knee pads and split open his knee when he slid into some lighting tracks on the floor.

Opening on December 30, 1954, *House of Flowers* played for five months on Broadway. After the show ended, the twenty-four-year-old Ailey decided to stay in New York to take acting and dance classes with leading dancers and choreographers. This gave him the opportunity to learn from world-renowned artists such as Martha Graham (modern dance) and Karel Shook (ballet).

Considered a pioneer in modern dance, Graham had studied with Denishawn from 1916 to 1923. She went on to found her own company and develop a system of moving that emphasized the sharp contractions and releasing of muscles. Shook, a former dancer with the Ballet Russe de Monte Carlo, had established a dance studio in New York City, where he trained most of the top African-American dancers of the day.

At this time, not many dance teachers were willing to take nonwhite dancers as students. Shook was one of the few who trained African-American dancers— especially men—in classical ballet. Along with Arthur Mitchell, Shook founded the Dance Theatre of Harlem, the first permanent black ballet company in the United States.

While Ailey did not care much for many of the formal dance techniques he studied in New York, he had the opportunity to explore many different art forms. Later he said, "Even though I starved a lot, I became immersed in the dance world."[4]

Ailey also took advantage of the many cultural resources the city had to offer. At first he lived in the area called Greenwich Village, a haven for painters, writers, poets, actors, and musicians. He went to poetry readings and music concerts, saw films, and enrolled in acting classes with Stella Adler, a famous acting coach. At the Stella Adler Theatre, Ailey also studied speech, voice, makeup, and movement. His involvement in the theater opened the door to a number of

Broadway musicals and dramas and even appearances on television shows.

At that time, there were not many prospects for African-American performers in the United States. Most Broadway shows were cast with white actors and dancers. Still, the civil rights movement—an organized effort for equality for all citizens—was gaining ground. In 1954, the Supreme Court made a historic ruling in *Brown* v. *The Board of Education of Topeka, Kansas.* The Court decided that racially segregated schools did not provide an equal opportunity to all children. Up to that time, laws in many states allowed separate schools for blacks and whites. The Court declared that black children were placed in inferior schools and therefore denied access to an equal education. This decision opened the way for the desegregation of many other public facilities, too.

The next year, 1955, marked Rosa Parks's historic bus ride. Parks's refusal to give up her seat to a white man on a bus in Montgomery, Alabama, touched off a major protest by blacks in that city. Under the leadership of Martin Luther King Jr., the plight of African Americans in Montgomery received national attention, leading to the integration of city buses.

That same year, the color line was crossed in classical ballet. In 1955 Arthur Mitchell became the first African American to join a classical ballet company, the New York City Ballet, under the direction of George

Balanchine. Mitchell later recalled that while he was able to be the dance partner to white ballerinas on stages all over the world, he could not do so on programs televised during prime time in the United States. "Television stations in the South would refuse to carry the shows, and advertisers would not like that," he said.[5]

In 1957 Ailey got the opportunity to perform in the musical *Jamaica*. The legendary Lena Horne, whom Ailey had seen when he was a teenager in Los Angeles, starred in the production along with Ricardo Montalban. Ailey was thrilled to be the lead dancer. The choreography was so difficult and the steps so quick that the dancers complained about the exhausting rehearsals. Cristyne Lawson, one of Ailey's friends and fellow dancers in the show, said, "If you ever did it full-out you needed an ambulance to carry you out."[6]

It was an exciting time for Ailey. His childhood idol Lena Horne was starring in her first Broadway role— and he was in the cast. Horne had persistently worked to integrate the show. "I fought for a black stage manager, for mixing minority musicians from the union and for a multiracial show, with Asians, blacks, whites, Mexicans, Puerto Ricans," she said.[7]

Set on the imaginary Pigeon Island, *Jamaica* is a story about Savannah, a young Caribbean woman (Horne) who longs to go to New York City. The show opened on October 31, 1957, at the Imperial Theater

Alvin's distinct style and attention to detail was apparent in all of his choreographies.

in New York City. It played for a year and a half on Broadway, with 555 performances. *Jamaica* went on to receive seven Tony Award nominations, including a nomination for Best Musical. Horne and Montalban both garnered Best Actress and Best Actor nominations as well. In the reviews for *Jamaica*, critics took note of Ailey, who was often called the "dancing deer" because of his agility, speed, and muscular build.[8] Lena Horne nicknamed him the "Earth Man" because of the solid, earthy way he moved.

Because the show did not have Sunday performances, Horne threw parties for the cast members on Saturday nights. Ailey quickly made friends with many of the other African-American dancers in the show, and he recruited them for some dances he was creating on his own.

While performing in *Jamaica*, Ailey was allowed to use the theater for his own rehearsals. He spent his free time creating new dances and experimenting with new movements. He explained, "I had wearied of doing other people's concerts. . . . I was tired of being told what to do. I had my own ideas, and the time had come for me to make my own decisions."[9] He tapped into his "blood memories" of the Dew Drop Inn and the True Vine Baptist Church for inspiration.

The result was the premier performance given at the 92nd Street YM-YWHA in New York City on March 30, 1958. Ailey had been nervous about having his creations viewed by the sophisticated New York audience and New York critics. He need not have worried. The dance critics who saw the show wrote glowing reviews. Judging from the applause and standing ovation Ailey and his dancers earned that day, Ailey was on his way to becoming one of America's celebrated choreographers.

6

THE ALVIN AILEY
AMERICAN DANCE
THEATER

With Ailey's newfound success, he and his dancers were invited back to the Jacob's Pillow Dance Festival in the summer of 1959. Ted Shawn, who had disliked Ailey's work a few years earlier, now had nothing but praise. Later that summer, the Ailey dancers were asked to represent the United States at the World Dance Festival in New York City.

With these heady triumphs under his belt, Ailey decided he was ready to form his own dance company, one that would showcase the black experience.

□□□

"The original idea," he said, "was to make a company where I could dance and where I could make up my own steps. And of course to say something about black material. About what had been contributed to American and world culture by black dance and music, poetry and drama. But mainly dance."[1]

Ailey founded his dance company in 1960. It would not carry the name Alvin Ailey American Dance Theater until a few years later. When the original group had performed in 1958 at the 92nd Street Y, the dancers were listed on the program as Alvin Ailey and Company and Ernest Parham and Company. Parham was a friend of Ailey's and a fellow Broadway dancer with whom Ailey collaborated. Before the company settled on its permanent name, it was known as Alvin Ailey, Carmen de Lavallade and Their American Dance Company.

Ailey said he started his own company for three reasons: (1) He wanted to give African-American dancers a chance to perform; (2) he dreamed of a multicultural dance company that could dance both classics and new works; and (3) he wanted to showcase the African-American experience through dance.[2] Ailey also gave other choreographers the chance to present their creations through his company. He believed that a dance company should showcase the works of many artists, not just its founder.

The first step was to find a studio. Ailey secured rehearsal space in the 51st Street YWCA's Clark Center

Alvin Ailey and his dance company gained worldwide fame.

for the Performing Arts, a building that had once been a grand hotel. The second floor of the building, which had been used for receptions, was perfect for the dancers. The rooms were large, with wood floors, and there was even a small theater. Ailey and his dancers flourished there. Ailey described it as "a lively place, a heaven, a wonderful center, especially for black dancers."[3]

In this supportive atmosphere, Ailey tapped into some of his earliest childhood memories and created *Revelations*. Using live singers and musicians, Ailey choreographed the piece to music that was central to the African-American experience: spirituals, gospel, blues, work songs, and folk songs. Music was very important to Ailey, who once said, "If the music doesn't work, the piece doesn't work."[4] Set in a small African-American church—the kind Ailey attended when he was a boy—*Revelations* reflects a wide range of human emotions that everyone can relate to. It proved to be a stunning success.

Revelations caught the attention of dance critics and the public alike. Even the U.S. State Department took note. In 1962 Ailey's dance company was invited to participate in President John F. Kennedy's Special International Program for Cultural Presentations. Soon Ailey and his dancers were serving as "cultural ambassadors" on five continents. The troupe traveled to Asia, Australia, Europe, Brazil, Africa, and the USSR. It was the first American dance company to tour the Soviet Union in fifty years. It was also the first black dance company funded by the U.S. State Department to tour Southeast Asia.

The original troupe was composed of ten dancers, all black. Then, in 1964, Ailey decided to integrate the company. He explained, "I felt that people were people and that a black theme expressed by dancers of all colors would be enlarged."[5] Ailey was criticized by those who felt that he should have kept the company all black. Ailey protested, saying, ""I think that having Japanese, white, Puerto Rican, Hawaiian, or whatever we have in the company, universalizes our material."[6]

As an adult, Alvin often created dances out of his childhood memories of rural Texas.

He explained, "I like to celebrate the difference. I mean, people are people. If somebody dances the blues a little differently, well, that's groovy."[7]

Ailey's determination to have a multiethnic dance company was part of Lester Horton's legacy. It was also one of Ailey's greatest gifts to the world of dance. Ailey once said, "I've always felt that I wanted to celebrate the differences in people. I didn't want all the same bodies, or all the same color, in my company."[8] According to choreographer Bill T. Jones, "Ailey claimed all styles and traditions of dance to be his own as an American citizen. That is a pretty big claim and part of his great contribution to dance."[9]

In 1964 the troupe embarked on its first tour of Europe. Throughout the tour, the dancers performed before packed concert halls and received enthusiastic applause and standing ovations. In Hamburg, Germany, they received sixty-one curtain calls—something that no dance company had ever achieved there. The troupe enjoyed similar receptions throughout Europe.

Although he still enjoyed dancing, Ailey stopped performing in 1965 and threw himself into choreographing, overseeing rehearsals, and raising funds for the company. He explained, "The reason I stopped was to get myself out of the middle of the stage, to let some of the young people who were hanging in the back come forward. . . . I think it comes from Lester Horton. I never really saw myself as the lead dancer of the company. I always saw myself as the person who was guiding, who was choreographing, who was making things happen for the younger people."[10]

Another reason Ailey stopped performing is that he needed time to aggressively seek funding for the company. One of his strategies was to make each season's opening night very special. Often he would unveil a distinctive new ballet. Other times, he would have a special guest artist—such as the ballet star Mikhail Baryshnikov—dance a new piece choreographed especially for the occasion. Ailey also made sure there was a big opening-night party. Tickets for opening night and the party were expensive. Wealthy patrons had such a good time that many of them later donated money to the company.

Some of Ailey's dancers reported that he was a perfectionist who would work them relentlessly until a dance was to his liking. Dudley Williams, a former dancer and teacher with Ailey's company, said that although Ailey could be gruff at times, he made many personal sacrifices for the sake of his company. "Ailey lived simply and was a rough man," said Williams. "His first allegiance was to the company. When he performed in a Broadway show he saved his money and put it back into the company. He sometimes financed a young choreographer from his own pocket."[11]

Ailey's friends almost always commented on his generosity. Ailey dancer James Truitte—who went on to become a dance professor and taught the Horton technique—said, "He was a complicated person and in constant flux, but being a friend is what he did best."[12] Ailey's friend Carmen de Lavallade described him as an unselfish spirit: "He gave you an open chest of gems, of jewels."[13]

John Parks was in the Ailey company from 1970 to 1974. Today he is a professor of dance at the University of South Florida. He first saw the company on a Sunday-morning television show called *Lamp unto My Feet*. Parks said he was "awed by the number of black people dancing" and the "spirit and energy." Parks attended his first Ailey performance in 1969, at Clark Center. "The attention to detail and their artistry really excited me. I was also intimidated by them," said Parks.[14]

When Ailey had first asked Parks to join the company, Parks turned him down. Everyone was a soloist, everyone was an individual, and all contributed to the makeup of the company in a tangible way. "I didn't see where I could fit into that," Parks said later. At the time, he told Ailey, "I have a few things I need to learn."[15] The next year, in 1970, Parks learned that Ailey was looking for more dancers. Parks showed up at the open audition and was hired on the spot.

Parks also said that Ailey was "very keen on communicating with kids." From the time the studio opened, Ailey had a children's program. While he was in the company, Parks did a lot of teaching. Ailey worked with disabled students, primarily children. Many were deaf or blind. Dance was a kind of therapy for them. "It was beautiful to see," said Parks.[16]

The Alvin Ailey American Dance Theater also fostered and promoted dance in areas where there was no dance. Often, the company would book engagements in cities and in theaters where other dance companies refused to perform. Ailey's dance groups regularly performed at schools, too. He wanted all children to have the opportunity to experience professional dance. Sometimes Ailey chartered a bus to bring in children to see a performance. He also made sure that Wednesday matinees were reserved for kids. Ailey once said, "It has always been one of my fantasies to have a school like the Horton school where I started, where everything was outgoing and natural and didn't make anybody feel like a freak because he wanted to be a dancer."[17]

Ailey's dream for a school came true in 1969. When the Ailey School first opened in Brooklyn, New York, it was called the Alvin Ailey American Dance Center and had about 125 students. Today, enrollment has increased to about 3,500 students. They study a wide range of dance techniques, including modern dance, ballet, Afro-Caribbean dance, jazz, tap, and the Horton technique, named after Ailey's mentor. Students may be as young as three years old. Junior-division students range from three to fifteen years old, and the professional division is for ages fifteen and older.

Denise Jefferson, director of the Ailey School, holds auditions throughout the United States. "To Alvin it was always terribly, terribly important to have an open admission policy. Everybody could study there, all races, and indeed we saw that. It was a wonderful place to be a young dancer."[18]

Jefferson recalled that Ailey liked to show up for surprise visits to the school. Sometimes he asked students to sit in a circle and share their dreams and career goals. Even though he posed challenging questions and pushed the students to dig deep for answers, he also offered support, guidance, and advice.[19] One of his friends said that of all the things Ailey had accomplished, "what gave him the most satisfaction was bringing his dance to the people, especially the children."[20]

Ailey also recognized a need to provide stage experience for his most talented students. So in 1974 he created the Alvin Ailey Repertory Ensemble to travel and perform in cities around the world. The group's touring lineup includes classic company works as well as new, experimental dances.

Another Ailey program for children grew out of Ailey's choreography. In 1984, he created a piece called *For Bird, with Love* in honor of the jazz great Charlie "Bird" Parker. This gifted but troubled saxophonist had died at the age of thirty-four as a result of his addiction to alcohol and heroin. Ailey's work, set to expressive jazz music, reflects a wide range of human emotion. In choreographing *For Bird, with Love*, Ailey developed close bonds with Parker's birthplace, Kansas City, Missouri. That association led to AileyCamp.

AileyCamp is an intensive, six-week summer program for kids ages eleven to fourteen. It began in 1988 in Kansas City to serve underprivileged children, free of charge. Today, AileyCamps can be found in Chicago, New York, Boston, and Kansas City. Students take classes in modern dance, jazz, ballet, and creative writing. Although children learn and practice dance, the goal of AileyCamp is not to train them to be professional dancers. Rather, the program urges them to excel through "the four A's: acceptance, attention, appreciation, and affection."[21] Through dance, students are encouraged to develop creativity, critical thinking, and self-esteem.

Looking back on his accomplishments, Ailey once said: "It's become much more enormous than I ever would have dreamed of back in the '50s. I never even thought I'd have a company of my own, much less something of this dimension."[22]

After moving around over the years, the Alvin Ailey American Dance Theater settled in 1989 on West Sixty-first Street, near Lincoln Center in New York City. The 77,000-square-foot building is the largest facility in the United States dedicated to dance.

Revelations is Alvin Ailey's masterpiece.

7

REVELATIONS

ance critics have said that never has the history of African Americans been better dramatized than in the Alvin Ailey American Dance Theater.[1] Perhaps no piece in Ailey's repertoire does this as well as the ballet *Revelations*. Ailey's tenth ballet has been called "the signature piece of the company and one of the most renowned dance compositions of the century."[2] It is considered a modern masterpiece by professional dance critics and dance lovers alike.

Revelations is not just one dance but rather several related dances put together into one piece.

Choreographed to African-American spiritual and gospel music, the dance celebrates southern black culture and religion. Ailey used a wide range of dance styles, including ballet, jazz dance, African movements, and modern dance.

Revelations has been captivating audiences since its debut performance on January 31, 1960, in the same YM-YWHA auditorium where Ailey and his dancers had first performed two years earlier. From the striking opening image of brown-hued dancers, arms outstretched, to the final scene of the piece, the audience at the Y in 1960 sat in stunned silence. At the curtain call, the dancers took their bows, anxiously awaiting a reaction from the audience. When the applause finally came, it was "deafening."[3]

Revelations is often danced as the closing piece of an Ailey program. At first it was ninety minutes long, but over the years it has been adjusted and modified. It is now about a half hour long. The dance critic David Vaughan has said, "The Ailey company without *Revelations* is almost unthinkable: each season, in fact, they attempt to make programs without it but . . . the public demand is such that they have to rearrange everything to put it on every night."[4] Judith Jamison, a former principal dancer with Alvin Ailey, said of *Revelations*, "It's a ballet about people who survive . . . it's universal and it's accessible."[5]

In *Revelations*, the dancers move the audience from

sorrow to rebirth to the final emotions of celebration and joy. The ballet is composed of three sections with several dances in each. The first part is often called the "brown" section because of the dancers' costumes. The second, "white" segment, suggests water and focuses on baptism and rebirth. Finally, the golden "yellow" section is joyful and celebratory. Although the ballet has evolved and changed through the years, the arrangement of the piece has remained constant:[6]

PILGRIM OF SORROW

I Been 'Buked

Didn't My Lord Deliver Daniel

Fix Me, Jesus

TAKE ME TO THE WATER

Processional/Honor, Honor

Wade in the Water

I Want to Be Ready

MOVE, MEMBERS, MOVE

Sinner Man

The Day Is Past and Gone

You May Run On

Rocka My Soul in the Bosom of Abraham

Much of the power of *Revelations* comes from the music. Ailey said that as a young boy he had been fascinated with the gospel songs and spiritual music played in small black churches throughout Texas.[7] To add to his childhood memories, Ailey also did extensive research, contacted experts in gospel and black spiritual music, and arranged for live singers as he created the work.

Revelations opens dramatically with the gospel piece "I Been 'Buked," which had been sung at Ailey's baptism. Dancers stand and lunge closely together, arms outstretched as if a flock of birds is getting ready to take flight. Each dancer is outfitted in brown jersey—a flexible fabric—dyed to match individual skin tones. John Parks, former Ailey dancer, noted that two of the many theatrical influences Ailey inherited from Lester Horton were "a sense of how fabric moves" and the importance of costumes.[8]

In the second section, "Take Me to the Water," dancers use long, flowing white and blue cloths to suggest a river. These water images are reminiscent of the small towns in which Ailey grew up, where baptisms would take place at a nearby lake or river. The dancers' undulating movements, too, suggest rippling water and its cleansing effect.

The final part, "Move, Members, Move," includes "The Day Is Past and Gone." For this piece, chairs are arranged as if they were pews in a church. The women dancers are outfitted with golden wide-brimmed hats and fluttering fans, and the audience can feel the strength of these African-American church ladies. It is easy to envision them exchanging a little gossip and humor before taking their places for the church service.

The finale of *Revelations* is the spirited "Rocka My Soul in the Bosom of Abraham." This joyful number brings the ballet to a close. Every time it is danced, the audience members are moved to clap, stomp, and vocally respond as if they were at a gospel church service. At one performance in Athens, Greece, six thousand audience members stood up and cheered for twenty minutes.[9] One of the compelling aspects of Ailey's choreographies, said John Parks, is that the audience becomes a "willing participant." For many audience members, "it's not just entertainment, it is food, therapy for them," he added.[10]

Many of Ailey's ballets have been danced by other companies, but *Revelations* is done only by Ailey's company. The single exception was made in 1968 when the Mexican Ballet Folklórico performed *Revelations* at the opening ceremonies of the Olympic Games. Explaining that the ballet is a statement about the African-American experience, Ailey has said, "I'm not so sure that it would work [for a white company]. Certainly the personal identification would not be there."[11]

The piece has become a sort of initiation for the members of the Ailey company. It has been said that it is only after his or her first *Revelations* performance that a dancer truly feels like a member of the Alvin Ailey American Dance Theater.[12]

Ironically, the overwhelming success of *Revelations* also proved to be a burden for Ailey. He had difficulty creating other pieces that had the same intensity and popularity.[13] As one dance critic wrote, "The problem with creating a masterpiece right out of the gate is that you spend the rest of your life trying to top it."[14]

According to Parks, one of the strategies that Ailey used to keep the dances fresh and the dancers interested in his works was to give the dancers different roles from night to night. This familiarized them with one another's perspectives of the dance. There were also several variations of each piece. For example, there were three versions of "Sinner Man" in *Revelations*. A different one would be danced from night to night. Parks feels that switching the dancers' roles "keeps the dance alive, heightens the passion, and helps develop the characters."[15]

To this day, *Revelations* remains Ailey's signature work—the piece he is best known for. It is estimated that by the late 1980s, *Revelations* had been performed more times than the famous ballet *Swan Lake*. Even when Ailey wanted to "rest" *Revelations*, audiences would not let him.[16] It is the public's favorite ballet in the Ailey repertoire. The critical and popular acclaim garnered by *Revelations* paved the way for funding, support, and recognition. It is now considered an American classic, and it helped to establish the Alvin Ailey American Dance Theater as one of the major companies in modern dance.

8

CRY

ancer Judith Jamison had first seen Alvin
Ailey in 1963, when the company performed
in her hometown of Philadelphia. Then, in
1965, Alvin Ailey sat in on an audition for a television
show that featured the singer Harry Belafonte. There
were many young women trying out that day. One
dancer in particular, Judith Jamison, caught Ailey's
eye. Ailey noticed that while all the other young
women were wearing fancy costumes and makeup,
Jamison "looked rather plain in a black leotard and
tights, which made her stand out from the others."[1] He
was awed by her long, strong legs.

Three days later, Ailey called Jamison and invited her to join his dance company. She went directly over to his dance studio. "I walked into Alvin's company like putting on a size fifty shoe. Everyone was a star. I was so nervous that I could hardly think. But I had no time to think," she said.[2] With Ailey's encouragement, she became a member of his troupe.

Although they respected each other very much, at first there was tension between Ailey and Jamison. Their strong personalities led to conflicts over the music and the choreography. Ailey was demanding of everyone in his company. Jamison, in her autobiography, later wrote: "He was idealistic and committed, and that made him hard to work with, and for. Alvin did not spare himself. He saw no reason to spare other people."[3] The friction lasted for about five years, until Ailey choreographed a piece that brought the two together.[4]

In 1971, on his mother's birthday, Ailey debuted *Cry*, a solo choreographed specifically for Jamison. It was a gift to his mother. Lula was thrilled and proud that her son had reflected her life in a dance: "I *did* cry but it made no difference how hard you worked, you could get up and dance. Made no difference how I could scrub floors. I could always get up and shimmy in the shoulders."[5]

In *Cry*, which is set to songs by Alice Coltrane, Chuck Griffin, and Laura Nyro, Ailey celebrates women's strength and determination. He dedicated it to "all black women everywhere, especially our mothers." Though the Ailey dance troupe is integrated, only African-American dancers perform *Cry*.

Jamison turned out to be the perfect dancer for the piece. She once described herself as "a dancer who happens to be a woman, who happens to be black." She said, "I guess the three things: dancing, femininity and blackness, make up who and what I am. I have never tried to separate them because if I did I would be fragmented, maybe shattered."[6] Dance professor John Parks believes that by allowing the dancers to retain their individuality, Ailey helped develop his dance pieces.[7] Many credit *Cry* with making Jamison a star in the world of dance. She usually received standing ovations for her performance.

In *Cry*, the lone female dancer is dressed completely in white. A long-sleeved leotard is paired with a low-slung, enormous white skirt. The dancer also uses a long white scarf as a prop. During the intense, sixteen-minute piece, the scarf is transformed from an infant's blanket to a scrub rag to a shawl to a regal turban. In Jamison's interpretation, the first part of the dance celebrates life, the second reflects many hardships African-American women endure, and the final section celebrates women's strength.[8]

As with other dances inspired by Ailey's childhood memories, *Cry* grew out of a variety of experiences. For example, the image of the shawl as a scrub rag evolved from Ailey's memories of seeing his mother on her hands and knees scrubbing floors.[9] Jamison said, "I think that Alvin tried to get rid of all the hurt, all the ugly degradation and humiliation [of black women] in *Cry*."[10]

It is a physically demanding solo piece. Eventually, an alternate dancer also learned the role because it was too strenuous for Jamison to perform at every concert. At one point, when Jamison's alternate, Consuela Atlas, had left the company, Jamison performed the piece twenty-eight consecutive times. Because of the many head rolls in the dance, she injured her spine.[11] Jamison said, "After you see someone do *Cry*, if you're backstage when she finishes, she's flat-out on the floor gasping for breath. But when the curtain goes up for the bow, you pull your nerves together quickly as if you haven't been in a collapsed state—winded, sweating, tired—two seconds before."[12]

Ailey also had the opportunity to collaborate on a ballet with one of his childhood idols, Duke Ellington. In 1970, the two men created *The River* for the American Ballet Theatre. Ellington composed the music, and Ailey choreographed the dance. *The River* has many references to water, with sections titled "Bubbling Rapids," "The Lake," and "Two Cities" (located on opposite banks of the river). Ellington

Alvin created *Cry* especially for Judith Jamison, above.

▣▣▣▣▣▣▣▣▣▣▣▣▣▣▣▣▣▣▣▣▣▣▣▣▣▣▣▣▣▣▣▣▣

finished composing all the music, but he died before the ballet was staged.

Later, in 1974, the company paid tribute to the jazz great with a Duke Ellington festival, called *Ailey Celebrates Ellington*. This successful affair showcased Ailey's talents as well as the musical legacy of Duke Ellington. The festival featured many of the dances that Ailey had choreographed to the jazz musician's music. Ellington's son, Mercer, directed the Ellington Orchestra, making the event extra special. Ailey said of his idol, "I loved him, I was stunned by him, I was inspired by him."[13] The festival, held at the New York State Theater in New York City, included performances of *The River*, *The Mooche*, *Night Creature*, *Reflections in D*, and *Pas de Duke*.

Pas de Duke was created in 1976 especially for Judith Jamison and the ballet star Mikhail Baryshnikov, who had defected from the Soviet Union just two years earlier. Although Baryshnikov was an accomplished classical ballet dancer, he was not prepared for the difficult modern dance and jazz moves of Ailey's choreography. In the end, the duet was a beautiful contrast of dance styles and highlighted both dancers' training and talent to great effect.

That same year, Ailey received the prestigious Spingarn Medal from the National Association for the Advancement of Colored People (NAACP). This award is given annually for outstanding achievement by an

African American. Other notable African Americans who have received the medal include Martin Luther King Jr., George Washington Carver, Rosa Parks, and Bill Cosby. Ailey's considerable contributions to the world of dance had already been recognized with several honorary doctorate degrees, presented to him by Princeton University, Adelphi University, and Bard College.

Despite all of Ailey's accomplishments, those who knew him best often characterized the choreographer as being filled with self-doubt. In an interview, he confessed, "I am a person who has never completely escaped from the scars of my childhood. Racism, which leaves a shadow on one's sense of accomplishment, can make one feel like a perpetual outsider, and even now, after creating over 150 ballets, I still sometimes have doubts."[14] He admitted, "I felt that no matter what I did, what ballet I made, how beautifully I danced, it was not good enough."[15]

Ailey was stressed by the constant pressure to create perfection: "This is such a terribly frustrating profession. It's a high-anxiety business. Dancing is either right or wrong, there's no in-between, so we're constantly living with the anxiety of trying to keep our standards up. The goal always seems to be just beyond us because we're always trying for the perfect statement."[16]

Ailey was also frustrated by criticism that his

company was at times too commercial and not artistic enough. Some people felt that some of the Ailey troupe's new dances looked like the big production numbers staged in Las Vegas nightclubs. Judith Jamison explained, "Alvin said that dance should not be an elitist experience but delivered back to all people, since it began with them."[17]

While he seemed to be outgoing, Ailey could also be painfully shy. Although he was an eloquent speaker by all accounts, close friends say that he had a deep fear of public speaking.[18] One of his friends described him as "quiet, dignified, eloquent, educated, traveled, regal, yet so very, very private, so very, very human."[19]

Although he had many friends, Ailey was known to be reclusive. Carmen de Lavallade, his good friend and dance partner, once said, "I don't think any of Alvin's personal friends ever really knew him, his background, where he came from, whether he had any family at all."[20] James Truitte, one of his closest friends, remarked, "He was one of the most complex, unpredictable, brooding, indecisive and, at times, one of the most animated persons who lived on this earth. Being a friend to Alvin was a constant challenge, for you never knew which complexity or personality you would encounter from day to day."[21]

Part of what might have contributed to Ailey's feelings of isolation was the fact that he was a homosexual. It was not easy being a gay man during the time

Ailey grew up. Ailey said that touring for six months a year did not allow time for maintaining personal relationships or a family life. One dance scholar believes that because Ailey saw his professional accomplishments constantly evaluated on the basis of his race, he avoided additional judgment by keeping his sexual identity private.[22] Only his closest friends knew about that part of his life.

In 1979, Joyce Trisler, a friend of Ailey's since their Horton studio days, died at the age of forty-five. When Ailey heard this news, he became very depressed. He was frightened by the prospect of dying an early death all alone in his apartment, as Joyce had. He decided, he said, to "live quickly and get all that I could from what time I had left."[23]

The loss of his close friend and the weight of professional pressures led Ailey to drugs, and he suffered a nervous breakdown, shouting uncontrollably in an apartment house lobby.

Ailey decided not to try to hide the incident. He instructed the company's publicist to tell reporters the truth.

The following year Ailey was admitted to a psychiatric hospital in New York. He was diagnosed with bipolar disorder, also called manic-depression. It is a condition characterized by wild mood swings. Ailey was able to get the help he needed, and he stopped abusing drugs, started taking prescribed medication,

Alvin suffered a breakdown after his longtime friend Joyce Trisler, above, died at the young age of forty-five.

and lost the weight he had gained after he stopped dancing. With his health back in order, he started working again. Later, he said of his breakdown, "I realize that ultimately it had the positive effect of forcing me to slow down and regroup personally, publicly, and artistically."[24]

Ailey explained, "I didn't know what was wrong with me—or that anything was. I understand better now. In part it was the death of [choreographer] Joyce Trisler at forty-five. My comrade. I thought to myself, 'And I'm forty-nine.' I suddenly had to live, and I plunged into everything—the school, fund raising, the board, tours, finding fault everywhere, seeing the dark instead of the light."[25]

With his regained health and renewed optimism, Ailey was on his way to even more achievements.

9

"GOING HOME"

I n 1988 Alvin Ailey received the prestigious
Kennedy Center Honor Award for his
extraordinary contribution to American
culture and achievement. Past honorees had included
notable artists and entertainers such as comedians
Lucille Ball and Bob Hope, opera singer Beverly Sills,
pianist Arthur Rubenstein, and singer Frank Sinatra.
Ailey was thrilled to receive an honor that had also
been given to several of the people he admired,
including Lena Horne, Arthur Mitchell, Martha
Graham, and Katherine Dunham.

Some people observed that Ailey did not look well,

but members of his company who saw him frequently did not seem to notice.[1] Ailey's body was by now giving him signs that it was failing. He often did not feel well, and his energy lagged. In the spring of 1989 he asked Judith Jamison to take over as director of his beloved company. Meanwhile, Paul Szilard, the company's international booking agent, had been prodding Ailey to seek medical advice. Szilard recommended his own doctor. Ailey dragged his feet, saying that he already had a doctor and was fearful of what might be found. But Szilard persisted, and after a year Ailey finally made an appointment with Szilard's doctor. Ailey was diagnosed with pneumonia, a destructive virus known as CMV, and an ulcer in his esophagus.[2]

During the summer of 1989, although Ailey's health was already declining, he traveled to Kansas City. He wanted to see the impact of AileyCamp, the program he had started for disadvantaged youth. He was amazed by what he saw. Rather than a typical, amateur children's recital, Ailey was impressed and touched to see children moving with confidence and style.[3] Sadly, this recital was to be one of his last public appearances.

Ailey was fifty-eight years old when he died on December 1, 1989, at Lenox Hill Hospital in New York City. His physician, Dr. Albert Knapp, reported that Ailey had been suffering from dyscrasia for about a year before his death. Dyscrasia is a rare blood disorder that affects a person's red blood cells and bone marrow. It is a condition often associated with HIV. Most sources today conclude that Ailey died of HIV complications.[4]

Ailey's memorial service, held in New York City in St. John the Divine Cathedral, was titled "A Celebration of Alvin Ailey Jr.: Going Home." The enormous Episcopal church had been the site of funerals for other well-known African Americans, including the writer James Baldwin and the musician Duke Ellington.

The service for Ailey, attended by 4,500 people, featured performances by his dance company. The coffin was covered in a rich red and purple cloth and placed at the foot of a makeshift stage. Later, Ailey's body was flown to California and buried at Rose Hills Memorial Park. He left most of his $750,000 estate to his mother. Personal items such as art, books, and a grand piano were left to various friends.

The drummer Max Roach played the funeral march. Lula Cooper, Ailey's mother, sat in front alongside her other son, Calvin. The mayor of New York City, David Dinkins, delivered a short but powerful eulogy, lamenting the loss of Ailey's creative genius. Ailey's longtime friend and dance partner Carmen de Lavallade also gave a moving speech, recollecting her friendship with Ailey as well as his many unique talents. Even President George H. W. Bush sent a message, describing Ailey as "a man of gentleness and vision."[5] Judith Jamison said, "Alvin Ailey radiated life. And dance was the prism through which he made visible the spectrum of our experiences."[6]

The funeral program included several of Ailey's works. *Song for You* was danced by Dudley Williams; a section from *Cry* was performed by Donna Wood (who had replaced Judith Jamison in the dance); and excerpts from *Revelations* were danced by two former company members, Mari Kajiwara and John Parks, along with current members of the company. John Parks, who also danced "Fix Me, Jesus" from *Revelations*, later said, "That was really moving. It was a very hard performance to do."[7] By the end of the performance, the entire audience had erupted into rhythmic clapping.

Before he died, Ailey had worked with A. Peter Bailey, a former editor of *Ebony* magazine, to record his autobiography. These recollections and interviews make up *Revelations: The Autobiography of Alvin Ailey*. It was published in 1995, a few years after Ailey's death.

Judith Jamison, the powerful dancer who had joined the company in 1965, was officially appointed Ailey's successor as artistic director of the Alvin Ailey American Dance Theater on December 20, 1989. At the appointment, Jamison spoke about her mentor: "He gave me legs until I could stand on my own, as a dancer and choreographer. I view this appointment

At Ailey's funeral, his longtime friend Maya Angelou depicted him as a "great tree."

as the course to take to continue my vision and to keep Mr. Ailey's legacy alive."[8] In her autobiography, *Dancing Spirit*, Jamison wrote, "I hope I'm a continuation of Alvin's vision. He has left me a road map. It's very clear. It works."[9]

One writer likened Ailey to a "great tree," saying, "He soaked up knowledge and inspiration from the culture that produced him, and produced leaves in the form of dances, branches that are the hundreds of dancers and choreographers who studied with him, performed with and for him, passed through his company and, ultimately, his school."[10]

This image of Ailey as a tree was also depicted at his funeral. Maya Angelou, who had been Ailey's friend since his brief time in San Francisco years earlier, composed a poem expressly for the occasion. In her tribute to Ailey, Angelou likened him to a tree so mighty that everything seems minor by comparison: "When great trees fall, rocks on distant hills shudder . . . Small things recoil into silence. . . ." She concluded by saying, "Lord, give him all the pliés he needs into eternity."[11]

10

THE AILEY
LEGACY

he Alvin Ailey American Dance Theater is considered to be not just a company, but a "school of thought."[1] In large part, this is because of Alvin Ailey's creative genius. Over the course of his relatively short career, Ailey created more than seventy-five original pieces. By combining African-American cultural elements with modern dance, Ailey created a unique dance form. For Ailey, inspiration for his dance works could be found everywhere from his memories of church services and honky-tonk bars to popular music such as jazz and blues. "Each movement is the sum total of moments and experiences," Ailey once said.[2] One dance critic noted how Ailey's childhood memories had influenced his two most popular pieces. "On Saturday night, everyone went to the Dew Drop Inn and sinned—that became 'Blues Suite.' On Sunday morning, they all went to church and repented—that was 'Revelations.'"[3]

Although Ailey created some very fine dances, many people feel that his legacy as a choreographer is not as important as his vision of a dance company. There simply is no other dance company like it. The Alvin Ailey American Dance Theater is unique in that it celebrates African-American culture with programs that are both artistic and enjoyable to a wide range of people.

In 1993, Jamison choreographed *Hymn* in Ailey's honor. Blending jazz, modern, and African dance styles, as well as her own background in classical ballet, Jamison used thirty-one dancers to depict memories and recollections of Ailey. The thirty-seven-minute work eventually became the centerpiece of a *Great Performances* program for public television (PBS). It is a beautiful tribute to an inspiring mentor.

Ailey is credited with helping people from all walks of life appreciate dance. The many tributes written after his death commented on his ability to bring dance to the people: "He was one of the few serious figures in dance . . . whose work was utterly accessible and loved by millions."[4] Keith McDaniel, a dancer with the Ailey company, agreed: "He made dance accessible to everyone. You didn't have to have a trained eye or read a book—all you had to do was open your heart. That's what Alvin was about, that spark of spirit."[5]

Alvin Ailey did not want dance to be an art form solely for the rich or well educated. "I still dream that my folks down on the farm in Texas can come to an Ailey concert and know and appreciate what's happening on stage," he said.[6]

Part of the reason all sorts of audiences have appreciated his dances is that they are colorful, full of energy, and theatrical. Ironically, these very characteristics also prompted criticism of Ailey's dances. Although some critics felt the dances were *too* entertaining, Ailey did not care. He said, "The Black pieces we do that come from blues, spirituals, and gospels are part of what I am. If it's art *and* entertainment—thank God, that's what I want it to be."[7]

One of the most often commented-upon aspects of Ailey's dance company is the multiethnic mix of the dancers. Ailey did not like the term "black dance." He said, "Good dance is good dance. It's not black or green or purple or white. Dance is just good or it's bad."[8] He once said that he hoped to show "that color is not important, that what is important is . . . a culture in which the young are not afraid to take chances and can hold onto their values and self-esteem."[9]

Ailey's legacy lives on today with the Alvin Ailey American Dance Theater.

Ailey's dances are universal because they go beyond languages and cultures.[10] The *New York Times* dance columnist Anna Kisselgoff wrote, "You didn't need to have known Ailey personally to have been touched by his humanity, enthusiasm, and exuberance and his courageous stand for multiracial brotherhood."[11]

The racism that persisted in the dance world disheartened Ailey. He lamented, "The dance world . . . is still a kind of closed society as far as Black dancers and choreographers are concerned. If we had to depend on it, very few Black dance artists of any kind would be working in the field."[12] Ailey was frustrated that in Europe his company was always well received, yet when the troupe returned to America there would be few engagements. Much of his time was spent trying to find funding to keep dance theater afloat financially.

Ailey was also concerned about the effects of racism on young people, the way it destroyed their self-confidence and self-esteem. He said that racism "tears down your insides so that no matter what you achieve, no matter what you write or choreograph, you feel it's not quite enough."[13] Ailey addressed this issue in social protest dances such as his 1969 *Masekela Langage*. In this piece about being black in South Africa, the dancers express the rage, frustration, and hopelessness of racism. Similarly, his 1986 work *Survivors* centered on the movement against apartheid, the South African system of racial segregation. Ailey said, "All my work, to some extent or other, is a cry against racism, against the injustice of that period."[14]

Today, the Alvin Ailey American Dance Theater continues to be a powerful force in the dance world. It is the only modern dance troupe to have more than thirty full-time dancers, year-round salaries, and a monthlong annual season at New York's City Center.[15] Many of Ailey's choreographies have been performed by other dance companies, too. The Dance Theatre of Harlem, the Joffrey Ballet, American Ballet Theatre, and the Paris Opera Ballet have all been graced by

Ailey's compositions. In an essay after his death, Judith Jamison wrote, "His contribution is fathomless."[16]

In 2004 the United States Postal Service issued a stamp series called American choreographers. Four great choreographers are honored: George Balanchine, Martha Graham, Agnes de Mille, and Alvin Ailey. The Ailey stamp features Ailey's face in three-quarter profile alongside a scene from *Revelations*.

It is has been said that more people have seen the Alvin Ailey American Dance Theater than any other American dance company.[17] Ailey's enduring legacy will continue to draw audiences and inspire new generations of dancers long into the future.

Chronology, with Selected Works

1931—Alvin Ailey Jr. is born to Alvin Ailey Sr. and Lula Elizabeth Ailey on January 5 in Rogers, Texas.

1937—Moves to Navasota, Texas.

1942—Moves to Los Angeles.

1945—Is greatly influenced by Katherine Dunham and her dance company.

1946—Lester Horton opens his dance school in Hollywood, California.

1949—Ailey begins studying dance with Lester Horton.

1950—Joins Lester Horton's dance company.

1953—Lester Horton dies suddenly of a heart attack; Ailey becomes artistic director of the company.

1954—Choreographs his first pieces, *According to St. Francis* and *Morning, Mourning,* in honor of his mentor, Horton.

1954—Appears in film *Carmen Jones;* performs on
–1957   Broadway in *House of Flowers; The Carefree Tree; Sing, Man, Sing;* and *Jamaica.*

1958—Has first public presentation at the Theresa Kaufman Auditorium of the 92nd Street YM-YWHA in New York City; presents *Blues Suite.*

1960—Founds his dance company, which later takes the name Alvin Ailey American Dance Theater (AAADT); *Revelations* debuts.

1961—Ailey choreographs *Roots of the Blues*.

1962—Is selected to participate in the president's Special International Program for Cultural Presentations and travels throughout the United States and the world; choreographs *Feast of Ashes* for the Joffrey Ballet.

1965—Stops performing; choreographs *Ariadne* for the Harkness Ballet (Ailey's first ballet on pointe), which premieres in Paris on March 12.

1966—Choreographs dance sequences in *Antony and Cleopatra* for the Metropolitan Opera's inaugural production at Lincoln Theater.

1967—Sponsored by the U.S. State Department, AAADT performs in ten African countries.

1969—The Alvin Ailey American Dance Center, Ailey's dance school in Brooklyn, is established; Ailey choreographs *Masekela Langage*.

1970—The AAADT becomes the first American dance troupe to tour the USSR; Ailey collaborates with the jazz musician Duke Ellington to create *The River* for American Ballet Theatre.

1971—*Cry* premiers; Ailey choreographs *Mass*, composed by Leonard Bernstein, to inaugurate the opera house of Kennedy Center in Washington, D.C.

1972—Receives honorary doctorate of fine arts from Princeton University; choreographs dance sequences in *Carmen* for the Metropolitan Opera.

1974—Alvin Ailey Repertory Ensemble, a touring dance company whose purpose is to enable the school's most talented students to gain stage experience, is established.

1975—Ailey receives the Dance Magazine Award; choreographs *Night Creature*.

1976—Is recognized with the New York City Mayor's Award of Arts and Culture and receives keys to the city; is honored with the NAACP's prestigious Spingarn Medal; choreographs *Pas de Duke* for Judith Jamison and Mikhail Baryshnikov.

1979—Is honored with the Capezio Award.

1982—Receives the United Nations Peace Medal.

1983—Creates *Au Bord du Précipice* for the Paris Opera Ballet, a ballet based on the life and early death of the rock star Jim Morrison.

1984—Choreographs *For Bird, with Love* for the late jazz great Charlie Parker.

1986—Choreographs *Survivors*, a biographical piece about Nelson and Winnie Mandela.

1987—Receives the Samuel H. Scripps American Dance Festival Award; AAADT stages *The Magic of Katherine Dunham*.

1988—Ailey receives Kennedy Center Honors Award and New York City's Handel Medallion for achievement in the arts.

1989—Receives Black Filmmakers Hall of Fame Award; dies on December 1 in New York City.

CHAPTER NOTES

Chapter 1. *Blues Suite*

1. Doris Hering, "Reviews," *Dance Magazine*, May 1958, p. 65.

2. C. S'thembile West, "Alvin Ailey: Signposts of an American Visionary," *Choreography and Dance*, vol. 4(1), 1996, p. 5.

3. Dudley Williams, as quoted in John Percival, "Going Back to His Roots," *The Independent*, June 14, 2002, p. 8.

4. Author interview with John Parks, Tampa, Florida, May 20, 2003.

5. Elizabeth Zimmer, *The Art of Belief*, PBS Online, <http://www-c.pbs.org/wnet/gperf/alvinailey99/meet.html> (November 6, 2002).

6. Judith Jamison, *Dancing Spirit* (New York: Doubleday, 1993), p. 71.

7. Hering, p. 65.

8. Don McDonagh, "Reflections of Ailey," *Dance Magazine*, December 1998, p. 56.

Chapter 2. The Birth of a Dancer

1. A. Peter Bailey, "Alvin Ailey Celebrates 30 Years of Dance," *Essence*, November 1988, p. 64.

2. Alvin Ailey, *Revelations: The Autobiography of Alvin Ailey* (New York: Birch Lane Press, 1995), p. 26.

3. Jennifer Dunning, *Alvin Ailey: A Life in Dance* (Reading, Mass.: Addison-Wesley Publishing Company, 1996), p. 4.

4. Ailey, p. 25.

5. Ibid., p. 18.

6. Bailey, p. 64.

7. Arthur T. Wilson, "A Million Roses Celebrating Champions," *Attitude* (*American Dance History* Supplement), Winter 1989, p. 39. Quoted Ailey in the *New York Times Magazine* (April 29, 1973).

8. Jacqueline Quinn Moore Latham, "A Biographical Study of the Lives and Contributions of Two Selected Contemporary Black Male Dance Artists," unpublished Ph.D. dissertation (Denton, Tex.: Texas Woman's University, 1972), p. 447.

9. Patrick Pacheco, "The Book of *Revelations*," *New York Daily News Magazine*, December 1988, p. 10.

10. Ailey, p. 35

11. Dunning, pp. 28–29.

12. Ailey, p. 36.

Chapter 3. Discovering Dance

1. Jennifer Dunning, *Alvin Ailey: A Life in Dance* (Reading, Mass.: Addison-Wesley Publishing Company, 1996), p. 32.

2. Alvin Ailey, *Revelations: The Autobiography of Alvin Ailey* (New York: Birch Lane Press, 1995), pp. 40–41.

3. A. Peter Bailey, "Alvin Ailey at the Met," *Ebony*, October 1984, p. 166.

4. Ailey, p. 43.

Chapter 4. Lester's Place

1. John Gruen, *The Private World of Ballet* (New York: Viking Press, 1975), p. 419.

2. Terrill Maquire, *York Dance Review*, Spring 1977, as quoted in Marjorie B. Perces et al., *The Dance Technique of Lester Horton* (Princeton, N.J.: Princeton Book Company, 1992), p. 7.

3. Bella Lewitzky, "A Vision of Total Theater," *Dance Perspectives*, Autumn 1967, p. 47.

4. Joan Pikula, "Celebrating Silver," *Dance Magazine*, December 1983, p. 46.

5. As quoted in Moira Hodgson, *Dance News*, April 1976, in C. S'thembile West, "Alvin Ailey: Signposts of an American Visionary," *Choreography and Dance*, vol. 4(1), 1996, p. 1.

6. Jacqueline Quinn Moore Latham, "A Biographical Study of the Lives and Contributions of Two Selected Contemporary Black Male Dance Artists," unpublished Ph.D.

dissertation (Denton, Tex.: Texas Woman's University, 1972), p. 477.

7. Gruen, p. 479.

8. Latham, p. 479.

9. Ibid., p. 480.

10. Ibid., p. 486.

11. Author interview with John Parks, Tampa, Florida, May 20, 2003.

12. Joseph H. Mazo, *The Alvin Ailey American Dance Theater* (New York: William Morrow and Company, 1978), p. 11.

13. "Prayer of St. Francis," <http://www.worldprayers.org/archive/prayers/invocations/lord_make_me_an_instrument.html> (May 1, 2004).

14. Ailey, p. 66.

15. Mazo, p. 11.

Chapter 5. On His Own

1. John Gruen, *The Private World of Ballet* (New York: Viking Press, 1975), p. 420.

2. Walter Terry, "Dance: Jacob's Pillow Festival," *Herald Tribune*, July 23, 1954, p. 14.

3. Jennifer Dunning, *Alvin Ailey: A Life in Dance* (Reading, Mass.: Addison-Wesley Publishing Company, 1996), p. 81.

4. Gruen, p. 421.

5. As quoted in Lynne Fauley Emery, *Black Dance: From 1619 to Today* (Princeton, N.J.: Princeton Book Company, 1988), p. 280.

6. Dunning, p. 97.

7. Ibid., p. 98.

8. Author interview with John Parks, Tampa, Florida, May 20, 2003.

9. Alvin Ailey, *Revelations: The Autobiography of Alvin Ailey* (New York: Birch Lane Press, 1995), p. 89.

Chapter 6. The Alvin Ailey
American Dance Theater

1. Alvin Ailey as quoted by Patricia Barnes, "Revelations: Alvin Ailey Talks to Patricia Barnes," *Ballet News*, November 1983, p. 15.

2. Thomas Faburn DeFrantz, *Revelations: The Choreographies of Alvin Ailey* (Ph.D. dissertation (New York: New York University, 1997), p. 41.

3. Alvin Ailey, *Revelations: The Autobiography of Alvin Ailey* (New York: Birch Lane Press, 1995), p. 93.

4. Hubert Saal, "Alvin Ailey's Black Power," *Newsweek*, December 29, 1980, p. 64.

5. Anna Kisselgoff, "Ailey: Dancing the Dream," *New York Times*, December 4, 1988, p. H1.

6. Barnes, p. 15.

7. John Gruen, *The Private World of Ballet* (New York: Viking Press, 1975), p. 423.

8. Joseph H. Mazo, *The Alvin Ailey American Dance Theater* (New York: William Morrow and Company, 1978), p. 13.

9. Robert Tracy, "Open Wide the Doors: Memories of a Mentor," *New York Times*, November 28, 1999, p. 39.

10. Barnes, p. 15.

11. As quoted in Muriel Topaz, "An Inside View of the Alvin Ailey American Dance Theater." *Choreography and Dance*, vol. 4(1), 1996, p. 16.

12. "Choreographer Alvin Ailey Touched Millions," *People Weekly*, December 18, 1989, p. 166.

13. Jennifer Dunning, "4,500 People Attend Ailey Memorial Service at St. John the Divine," *New York Times*, December 9, 1989, sec. 1, p. 31.

14. Author interview with John Parks, Tampa, Florida, May 20, 2003.

15. Ibid.

16. Ibid.

17. Barnes, p. 15.

18. K. C. Patrick, "Spotlight on Denise Jefferson," *Dance Teacher Now*, September 1989, p. 21.

19. Denise Jefferson, "Alvin Ailey and the Alvin Ailey American Dance Center," *Choreography and Dance*, vol. 4(1), 1996, pp. 24–25.

20. Allan S. Gray III, "Life with Alvin: A Kansas City Story," *Choreography and Dance*, vol. 4(1), 1996, p. 37.

21. Ronnie Favors, "AileyCamp," *Choreography and Dance*, vol. 4(1), 1996, p. 41.

22. Alan M. Kriegsman, "Alvin Ailey, Dancing on the Edge of High Anxiety," *Washington Post*, February 6, 1980, p. D7.

Chapter 7. *Revelations*

1. Hubert Saal, "Alvin Ailey's Black Power," *Newsweek*, December 29, 1980, p. 64.

2. Richard A. Long, *The Black Tradition in American Dance* (London: Prion, 1995), p. 144.

3. Jennifer Homans, "Revelations," *The New Republic*, April 22, 2002, p. 33.

4. Vaughan, 1975, as quoted in DeFrantz, p. 371.

5. Judith Jamison, Dancing Spirit (New York: Doubleday, 1993), p. 121.

6. Richard A. Long, *The Black Tradition in American Dance* (London: Prion, 1995), p. 144.

7. Alvin Ailey, *Revelations: The Autobiography of Alvin Ailey* (New York Birch Lane Press, 1995), p. 97.

8. Author interview with John Parks, Tampa, Florida, May 20, 2003.

9. Homans, p. 33.

10. Author interview with John Parks.

11. Sandler, 1978, as quoted in DeFrantz, p. 375.

12. Jamison, p. 116.

13. Homans, p. 36.

14. Elizabeth Zimmer, *The Art of Belief*, PBS Online,

<http://www-c.pbs.org/wnet/gperf/alvinailey99/meet.html>
(November 6, 2002).

15. Author interview with John Parks.

16. John Percival, "Going Back to His Roots," *The Independent*, June 14, 2002, p. 9.

Chapter 8. *Cry*

1. A. Peter Bailey, "Alvin Ailey Celebrates 30 Years of Dance," *Essence*, November 1988, p. 64.

2. Olga Maynard, "Judith Jamison," *Dance Magazine*, November 1972, p. 27.

3. Judith Jamison, *Dancing Spirit* (New York: Doubleday, 1993).

4. Alvin Ailey, *Revelations: The Autobiography of Alvin Ailey* (New York Birch Lane Press, 1995), p. 123.

5. Jennifer Dunning, *Alvin Ailey: A Life in Dance* (New York: Addison-Wesley Publishing Co., 1996), p. 271.

6. Olga Maynard, "Judith Jamison," *Dance Magazine*, November 1972, p. 27.

7. Author interview with John Parks, Tampa, Florida, May 20, 2003.

8. Jamison, p. 132.

9. Ailey, p. 32.

10. Maynard, p. 26.

11. Ibid., p. 29.

12. Jamison, pp. 135–136.

13. Don McDonagh, "Reflections of Alvin," *Dance Magazine*, December 1998, p. 60.

14. Bailey, p. 140.

15. John Percival, "Going Back to His Roots," *The Independent*, June 14, 2002, p. 9.

16. Alan M. Kriegsman, "Alvin Ailey, Dancing on the Edge of High Anxiety," *Washington Post*, February 6, 1980, p. D1.

17. Judith Jamison, "Missing Alvin Ailey as a New Era Dawns," *New York Times*, November 29, 1998, p. 11.

18. Allan S. Gray III, "Life with Alvin: A Kansas City Story," *Choreography and Dance*, vol. 4(1), 1996, p. 40.

19. Ibid.

20. Cecelie S. Berry, "Alvin Ailey: A Life Choreographed," *Emerge*, March 31, 1995, p. 60.

21. James Truitte, "Dear Alvin," *Choreography and Dance*, vol. 4(1), 1996, pp. 9–10

22. Thomas Faburn DeFrantz, *Revelations: The Choreographies of Alvin Ailey* (New York: New York University, 1997), p. 296.

23. Ailey, p. 135.

24. Bailey, p. 140.

25. Hubert Saal, "Alvin Ailey's Black Power," *Newsweek*, December 29, 1980, p. 64.

Chapter 9. "Going Home"

1. Dudley Williams, as quoted in Muriel Topaz, "An Inside View of the Alvin Ailey American Dance Theater," *Choreography and Dance*, vol. 4(1), 1996, p. 20.

2. Jennifer Dunning, *Alvin Ailey: A Life in Dance* (Reading, Mass.: Addison-Wesley Publishing Company, 1996), p. 391.

3. Ronnie Favors, "AileyCamp," *Choreography and Dance*, vol. 4(1), 1996, p. 43.

4. Dunning, p. 392.

5. Jennifer Dunning, "4,500 People Attend Ailey Memorial Service at St. John the Divine," *New York Times*, December 9, 1989, sec. 1, p. 31.

6. Judith Jamison, "A Letter from Judith Jamison," in Laura Beaumont, *Alvin Ailey American Dance Theater* (New York: McTaggart-Wolk, 1990), p. 1.

7. Author interview with John Parks, Tampa, Florida, May 20, 2003.

8. Laura Beaumont, *Alvin Ailey American Dance Theater* (New York: McTaggart-Wolk, 1990), p. 26.

9. Judith Jamison, *Dancing Spirit* (New York: Doubleday, 1993), p. 262.

10. Elizabeth Zimmer, The Art of Belief, PBS Online, <http://www.brislington.bristol.sch.uk/Curriculum_Pages/faculties/arts/Alvin%20Ailey.html> (November 6, 2002).

11. Maya Angelou, "Ailey, Baldwin, Floyd, Killens, and Mayfield," *I Shall Not Be Moved* (New York: Random House, 1990), p. 47.

Chapter 10. The Ailey Legacy

1. Anna Kisselgoff in a 1983 *New York Times* review, as quoted in C. S'thembile West, "Alvin Ailey: Signposts of an American Visionary," *Choreography and Dance*, vol. 4(1), 1996, p. 1.

2. Mindy Aloff, "Dancing with Death," *New York Times*, November 3, 1996, sec. 7, p. 13.

3. Joan Acocella, "The Brains at the Top," *New Yorker*, December 27, 1999–January 3, 2000, p. 139.

4. Death notices, *Newsweek*, December 11, 1989, p. 64.

5. Bill Steig, "Dancer, Choreographer Remembered," *Associated Press*, December 9, 1989.

6. Jennifer Homans, "Revelations," *New Republic*, April 22, 2002, p. 35.

7. Jennifer Dunning, "Alvin Ailey, A Leading Figure in Modern Dance, Dies at 58," *New York Times*, December 2, 1989, p. A1.

8. As quoted in Muriel Topaz, "An Inside View of the Alvin Ailey American Dance Theater," *Choreography and Dance*, vol. 4(1), 1996, p. 17.

9. "Choreographer Alvin Ailey Touched Millions," *People Weekly*, December 18, 1989, p. 166.

10. Author interview with John Parks, Tampa, Florida, May 20, 2003.

11. Anna Kisselgoff as quoted in "Pas de 'Duke'"; <http://www.abt.org/library/archive/choreographers/ailey_a.html> December 26, 2002.

12. A. Peter Bailey, "Alvin Ailey at the Met," *Ebony*, October 1984, p. 166.

13. Alvin Ailey, *Revelations: The Autobiography of Alvin Ailey* (New York: Birch Lane Press, 1995), p. 5.

14. Patrick Pacheco, "The Book of Revelations," *New York Daily News Magazine*, December 4, 1988, p. 11.

15. Elizabeth Zimmer, The Alvin Ailey American Dance Theater, PBS Online <http://www-c.pbs.ornet/gperf/alvinailey99/look.html> (November 6, 2002).

16. Judith Jamison, "Missing Alvin Ailey as a New Era Dawns," *New York Times*, November 29, 1998, p. 11.

17. Lynne Fauley Emery, *Black Dance: From 1619 to Today* (Princeton, N.J.: Princeton Book Company, 1988), p. 272.

FURTHER READING

Ailey, Alvin Jr., and A. Peter Bailey. *Revelations: The Autobiography of Alvin Ailey*. Bridgewater, N.J.: Replica Books, 1999.

Defrantz, Thomas F. Dancing *Revelations: Alvin Ailey's Embodiment of African American Culture*. New York: Oxford University Press, 2003.

Dunning, Jennifer. *Alvin Ailey: A Life in Dance*. New York: Perseus Book Group, 2000.

Fleming, Robert. *Alvin Ailey: Dancer/Choreographer*. Los Angeles, Ca.: Holloway House, 2002.

Ford, Carin T. *Legends of American Dance and Choreography*. Berkeley Heights, N.J.: Enslow Publishers, 2000.

Haskins, James. *Black Dance in America: A History Through Its People*. Thomas Y. Crowell: New York, 1990.

Kuklin, Susan. *Reaching for Dreams: A Ballet from Rehearsal to Opening Night*. Lincoln, Neb.: iUniverse, Inc., 2001.

Lewis-Ferguson, Julinda. *Alvin Ailey, Jr.: A Life in Dance*. New York: Walker and Company, 1994.

Mitchell, Jack. *Alvin Ailey American Dance Theater: Jack Mitchell Photographs*. Kansas City, Mo.: Andrews and McMeel, 1993.

Probosz, Kathilyn. *Alvin Ailey*. New York: Bantam Doubleday Dell Books for Young Readers. 1994.

Thorpe, Edward. *Black Dance*. New York: Overlook Press, 1994.

Internet Addresses

Alvin Ailey American Dance Theater
<http://www.alvinailey.org>

A Hymn for Alvin Ailey
<http://www.pbs.org/wnet/gperf/alvinailey>

Alvin Ailey biography
<http://www.topblacks.com/arts/alvin-ailey.htm>

Videos

A Tribute to Alvin Ailey. West Long Branch, N.J.: Kultur, 1990.

Going Home: Alvin Ailey Remembered. New York: WNET-Thirteen, 1989.

INDEX

Page numbers for photographs are in **boldface** type.